Designed For Success

Military Vehicles

Revised & Updated

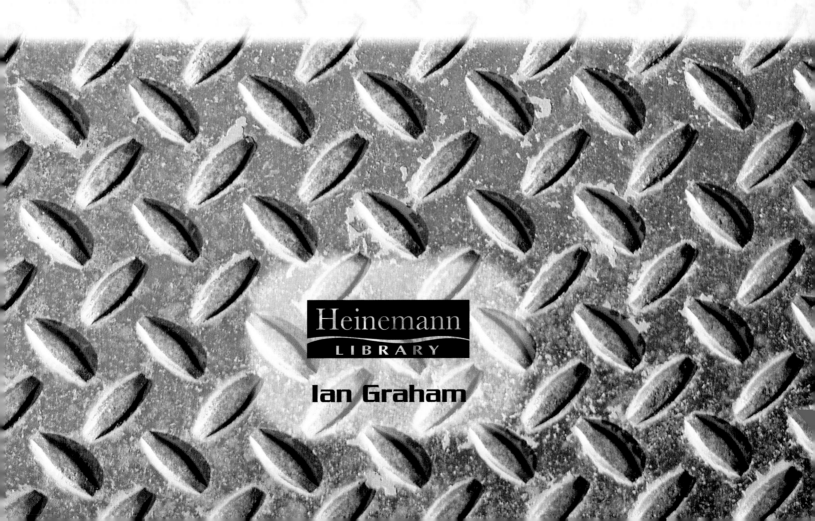

Heinemann
LIBRARY

Ian Graham

www.heinemann.co.uk/library

Visit our website to find out more information about **Heinemann Library** books.

To order:

☎ Phone 44 (0) 1865 888066

🖹 Send a fax to 44 (0) 1865 314091

🖥 Visit the Heinemann Bookshop at www.heinemann.co.uk/library to browse our catalogue and order online.

First published in Great Britain by Heinemann Library, Halley Court, Jordan Hill, Oxford, OX2 8EJ, part of Harcourt Education.
Heinemann is a registered trademark of Harcourt Education Ltd.

© Harcourt Education Ltd 2008
The moral right of the proprietor has been asserted.

Editorial: Andrew Farrow and Dan Nunn
Design: Steven Mead and Geoff Ward
Illustrations: Geoff Ward
Picture Research: Melissa Allison
Production: Alison Parsons

Originated by Modern Age
Printed and bound in China by South China Printing Company

ISBN 978 0 431 16579 0 (hardback)
13 12 11 10 09 08
10 9 8 7 6 5 4 3 2 1

ISBN 978 0 431 16587 5 (paperback)
13 12 11 10 09 08
10 9 8 7 6 5 4 3 2 1

British Library Cataloguing-in-Publication Data

Graham, Ian, 1953 –
  Military Vehicles. – (Designed for Success) 2nd edition
  1. Vehicles, military – Juvenile literature
  I. Title
  623.7'4
A full catalogue record for this book is available from the British Library.

Acknowledgements

The publishers would like to thank the following for permission to reproduce photographs:
© Aviation Picture Library p. **25** (top); © British Museum p. **28**; © Corbis/epa/Alaa Badarneh p. **4**; © Corbis/MPL/Peter Russell p. **9** (bottom); © Defense Visual Information Center p. **13** (top); © EPA p. **25** (bottom); © General Dynamics pp. **9** (middle), **13** (bottom), **26**; © Getty Images/Time Life Pictures/Timepix/Randy Jolly p. **8**; © Lockheed Martin p. **23** (bottom); © MPL p. **16**; © PA Photos/ Andrew Parsons p. **6**; © Popperfoto/Charles Platiau/Reuters p. **17** (top); Popperfoto/Jack Dabaghian/Reuters p. **11**; Popperfoto/Matko Biljak/Reuters p. **12**; © Popperfoto/Nikola Solic/Reuters p. **20**; © TRH Pictures pp. **3**, **5** (top), **7** (bottom), **15** (top), **17** (bottom), **19** (bottom), **21** (top), **21** (bottom), **23** (top), **24**; © TRH Pictures/A. Landau pp. **5** (middle), **5** (bottom); © TRH Pictures/Christopher F. Foss p. **7** (top); © TRH Pictures/GIAT Industries p. **27** (top); © TRH Pictures/IWM p. **29**; © TRH Pictures/US Department of Defense p. **22**; © TRH Pictures/E. Nevill pp. **18**, **19** (top), **27** (bottom); © TRH Pictures/General Dynamics p. **1**; © TRH Pictures/M. Ingram p. **14**; © TRH Pictures/M. Roberts p. **15** (bottom); © TRH Pictures/US Army pp. **9** (top), **13** (middle).

Cover photograph reproduced with permission of © Getty Images/ David Silverman. Background images by © istockphoto/Phil Morley and © Corbis.

Every effort has been made to contact copyright holders of any material reproduced in this book. Any omissions will be rectified in subsequent printings if notice is given to the publishers.

Disclaimer

All the Internet addresses (URLs) given in this book were valid at the time of going to press. However, due to the dynamic nature of the Internet, some addresses may have changed, or sites may have ceased to exist since publication. While the author and publishers regret any inconvenience this may cause readers, no responsibility for any such changes can be accepted by either the author or the publishers.

Contents

Any words appearing in the text in bold, **like this**, are explained in the Glossary.

MILITARY VEHICLES

Success in wartime depends on having powerful fighting forces. It also depends on being able to move troops, weapons, and supplies to the right place at the right time. This is the vitally important job of military vehicles.

Military forces use a wide variety of vehicles. Tanks, **self-propelled guns**, and rocket launchers are formidable mobile weapons. Trucks move troops and supplies. **Armoured personnel carriers (APCs)** and **light tanks** protect troops while they are moving around. **Reconnaissance** vehicles probe the land ahead of troops and spy on enemy forces. Recovery vehicles help other vehicles that have got into difficulty. Each is designed to do its own specialized job.

Leopard on the prowl ▽

The German Leopard 2 is one of the most fearsome military vehicles – a **main battle tank (MBT)**.

- The Leopard 2 is so solidly constructed and carries so much **armour** that it weighs an astonishing 62 tonnes. That is as much as 40 typical family cars!

- If it ran on ordinary wheels, it would sink into the ground. Instead, it runs on **tracks** that spread its weight over a greater area.

- A vehicle of this enormous weight needs an extremely powerful engine. The Leopard 2 is powered by a 1,500-**horsepower diesel engine**.

Borrowing from ▷ other designs

Not every new military vehicle is designed from scratch. Time and costs are saved by using parts that have already proved successful in other vehicles. The German Gepard anti-aircraft tank is built on the **chassis** (basic frame) of a Leopard MBT. **Radar** dishes on top of the turret search the sky for targets. The turret's twin guns are then trained on the approaching enemy aircraft.

◁ Troop transport

The US Bradley M2 Armoured Fighting Vehicle (AFV) is designed to transport troops safely in the thick of the action in combat. Each vehicle carries a crew of three, plus up to seven troops, at up to 66 kph (41 mph). Its body is made from **aluminium**, a very lightweight metal, covered by light armour. Two guns are mounted on a rotating turret. They are used to give **covering fire** for troops entering and leaving the vehicle.

BRADLEY M2 ARMOURED FIGHTING VEHICLE

Crew: 3

Length: 6.5 metres

Weight: 22.5 tonnes

Top speed: 66 kph (41 mph)

Armament:
25 mm gun anti-tank missile machine gun

Heavy movers △

Armies often need heavy construction and engineering vehicles. Some of these are also produced by modifying other vehicles. The US M-728 Combat Engineer Vehicle is a military bulldozer. It is based on a M60A1 MBT.

Battle tanks

Military vehicles are designed to work in some of the most difficult and dangerous conditions. The **main battle tank (MBT)** is one of the most important vehicles used in modern land warfare.

A tank designer has to strike a balance between firepower, crew protection, and mobility. Most tanks follow the same basic layout – an **armoured** hull riding on twin **tracks** with a rotating gun turret on top. The tank has to be big enough for a crew of three or four people to work inside. The commander is in overall control. A second crewman drives the tank. Two more, the gunner and loader, usually look after the main gun. Some tanks have an "auto-loader", a machine that replaces the loader. There must also be space to store the **shells** that the gun fires. The designer might choose to fit a bigger gun or thicker armour, but these would make the tank heavier and less mobile. Thinner armour would be lighter, but would offer less protection.

Challenger 2 ▽

Britain's main battle tank, the Challenger 2 MBT, is armed with a **stabilized gun**. The gun is kept steady and pointed at its target even when the tank turns or drives over rough ground. Unusually for tanks today, the gun has a rifled **barrel** – grooves spiral down inside its length. When a shell is fired down the barrel, the grooves make it spin. A spinning shell is more stable in the air and therefore more accurate.

CHALLENGER 2 MBT

Crew: 4

Length: 11.5 metres

Weight: 62.5 tonnes

Top speed: 59 kph (37 mph)

Armament:
120 mm main gun
7.62 mm chain gun
7.62 mm anti-aircraft gun

Exploding armour ▷

The Russian T-90 MBT is protected by one of the strangest types of armour used today. It's called Explosive Reactive Armour (ERA). It is actually designed to explode when an **artillery** shell hits it! By exploding, it stops the shell or anti-tank **round** from bursting through the tank's hull.

Tank without turrets △

The Swedish Stridsvagn (Strv) 103 has an unusual design. It has no gun turret. This makes it very low and more difficult for enemy tanks to hit. The gun is fixed in position. It can't be raised or turned. To aim, the tank is turned until it points in the right direction. Then the whole tank is tilted to raise the gun. The disadvantage of this design is that the gun can't be fired while the tank is moving. Sweden has now replaced its 103s with German Leopard 2 tanks.

Abrams M1A2 MBT
DESIGNED TO SURVIVE

The M1A2 is the latest version of the high-tech M1 Abrams tank. Designers made the Abrams tank flatter and lower than most other tanks. This makes it more difficult for enemy fire to hit it. The sides of its turret slope in at an angle to deflect bullets and rockets. If an anti-tank **round** hits the top of the tank, panels there are designed to explode outwards. This stops the round from bursting inside the tank. The M1A2's job is to attack the enemy head-on. Because it is most likely to be fired at from straight ahead, its designers put the thickest **armour** at the front. It is powered by a **gas turbine** engine (see pages 16–17).

Low profile

Designers wanted to keep the front of the Abrams M1A2 as low as possible. Therefore, the driver has to lie down on his back, like a racing driver, instead of sitting upright. The space is so cramped that there is no room for a steering wheel. Instead, the driver steers with a T-shaped bar, like motorcycle handlebars, between his knees. Twisting the right handgrip starts the tank moving. Turning the bar steers it. A pedal under the driver's right foot operates the brake.

The M1A2 Abrams is designed to be the best tank on any battlefield.

Sideskirts

A tank's wheels and **tracks** are the weakest part in its design. The turret and hull are heavily armoured, but the wheels and tracks are outside the armour and more easily damaged. If a tank's tracks or wheels become damaged, it cannot **manoeuvre** and it will soon be blown up by the enemy. The Abrams has armour-plated sideskirts fixed over the top half of the tracks to give them some protection.

Taking a view

A tank crew needs to be able to see outside the tank. However, in combat, the crew is sealed inside. The solution is to use **periscopes**.

- The commander of an Abrams M1A2 has six periscopes so he can look out in any direction.
- The driver has another three periscopes.
- The gunner has a viewfinder for looking at targets.

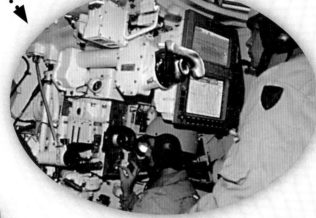

Night sight

The tank also has a thermal imaging system for seeing in dark or smoky conditions. This detects the heat that is given out by hot objects such as vehicle engines. The hotter an object is, the brighter it looks. Vehicles or guns that have stopped stay hot for a while. They, too, can be detected by the thermal system, even when they are hidden under **camouflage** netting or **foliage**, like the gun on the left.

CLOSER LOOK

Abrams M1A2 MBT CONSTRUCTION

An Abrams M1A2 MBT is built from more than 5,000 parts at a cost of more than US$4 million (£2.6 million). The tank is built in two main sections – the hull and the turret. The hull is cut from steel sheets up to 30 centimetres thick and **welded** together. The turret is made separately and then the two are fitted together.

Both the hull and the turret have to be made very accurately. They have to fit together closely enough to keep gas and other harmful chemicals and particles out of the tank. Air sucked into the tank for the crew to breathe is cleaned by filters. These remove all harmful or **radioactive** substances. Once the engine is fitted and all the electronic systems installed, the final job is to fit the tracks. Every Abrams M1A2 is then driven on a special test-track and its main gun is test-fired. Engineers check that everything works properly before each tank is handed over to the army.

Tracks

Each of the Abrams tank tracks is 15.2 metres long and made from 79 metal links, like a flattened bicycle chain. The tank's weight rests on tough rubber pads fitted to the links. These pads can be replaced when they wear out, instead of having to replace the whole link. They also increase grip and reduce noise when the tank is driven on roads. However, the rubber pads can't grip ice. Sometimes the tank has to operate on slippery surfaces. Then, the rubber pads on every fifth link are replaced by metal plates, called cleats, which can bite into the surface better.

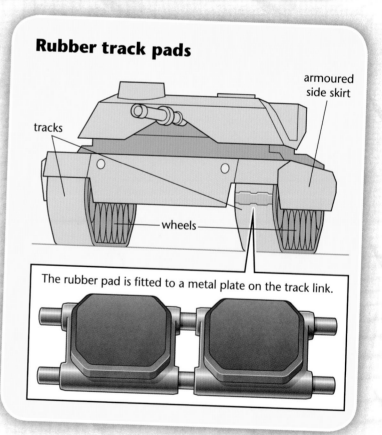

Rubber track pads

armoured side skirt

tracks

wheels

The rubber pad is fitted to a metal plate on the track link.

Armour

The design of a tank's armour is a closely guarded secret. The Abrams tank has armour made from **depleted uranium**, encased in steel. Depleted uranium is a waste product of the **nuclear** industry. It is used because it is a very **dense** metal. It blunts dart-shaped, anti-tank rounds and stops them from punching holes in the tank. The uranium is slightly radioactive. But, because it is encased in steel, the radiation level inside the tank is lower than the natural radiation in the outside world.

ABRAMS M1A2 MBT

Crew: 4

Length: 9.8 metres

Weight: 69.5 tonnes

Top speed: 67 kph (42 mph)

Armament: 120 mm main gun
7.62 mm machine gun
7.62 mm anti-aircraft gun
12.7 mm anti-aircraft gun

CLOSER LOOK

Abrams M1A2 MBT
FAST AND FURIOUS

The M1A2 is surprisingly agile for such a heavy vehicle. So what happens if an Abrams' tank driver opens the **throttle** and sets off as fast as possible? In less than six seconds, the 70-tonne vehicle is doing more than 30 kph (19 mph). In a few seconds more, it can be doing 67 kph (42 mph)! If it has to stop, its brakes are amazingly powerful. Under full braking, the tank can stop from 50 kph (31 mph) in about 3 metres! Its firepower is awesome, too. Its massive 120-mm gun can destroy six different targets up to 4 kilometres away within a minute.

Fire control

When an Abrams tank's crew spots a target:

- a **laser range-finder** fires an intense beam of light at it
- the time it takes for the reflection to bounce back is measured
- the tank's fire-control computer uses this time to calculate exactly how far away the target is
- the computer then calculates the gun's direction and elevation (how high it must be raised). It allows for wind speed, wind direction, and even the slightest bend in the gun **barrel**.

Within a few seconds of spotting a target, the gun is locked onto it and ready to fire.

Keeping cool

With all the hatches closed, the temperature inside a tank's cramped crew compartment soon soars. The Abrams M1A2 can therefore be fitted with a cooling system. This keeps the air temperature below 35° Celsius, and surfaces that the crew has to touch below 52° Celsius.

Abrams in action

During the 1991 Gulf War to liberate Kuwait from an Iraqi invasion, a tank force including 2,000 US Abrams tanks destroyed nearly 2,000 Iraqi tanks. Not a single Abrams tank was lost. The Abrams tanks could open fire when they were still about 1,000 metres beyond the range of Iraq's Soviet-made tanks.

In this picture, the damage done to an Iraqi tank by a US **shell** is clearly visible.

Smooth ride

The Abrams tank runs on seven wheels, but none of them are driven by the engine. The engine drives a pair of toothed wheels (called drive sprockets) right at the back of the tank. The teeth fit holes in the tracks and drive them round. The seven road-wheels support the weight of the tank. Each wheel is attached to a rod called a **torsion** bar that twists when the wheel is pushed up by a bump. The torsion bars behave like springs. They keep the tracks pressed down on bumpy, uneven ground while the tank glides along smoothly.

CLOSER LOOK

Designing for war

Military vehicles are designed according to the jobs they have to do. As we have seen, **main battle tanks**, the biggest tanks on a battlefield, are very heavy because of their massive **armour**. However, **armoured personnel carriers (APCs)** and **light tanks** are made small and **manoeuvrable**. This means they can move around nimbly and quickly before heavy weapons can be brought to bear on them.

Designers have to think about many other things too. How are their vehicles going to be transported? Are they light enough to be lifted by helicopter? Will they fit inside a transport plane? Can they travel on public roads under their own power or will they need to be towed on trailers? The cost of producing each vehicle is another important factor.

STORMER 30 LIGHT TANK

Crew: 3

Length: 5.25 metres

Weight: 13 tonnes

Top speed: 80 kph (50 mph)

Armament: 30 mm cannon
2 x machine guns
2 x grenade launchers
optional missile launcher

Going to war ▷

Military vehicles often have to travel long distances. Their designers have to make sure that they can be carried by other transport vehicles. The British Stormer armoured vehicle can be airlifted by a Sikorsky CH-53 helicopter or inside a Lockheed C-130 transport plane. It can also be carried by trucks and by rail. It can even be landed from the sea using **amphibious** landing craft.

Crew safety ▷

Designing a vehicle to give its crew maximum protection is not simply a matter of surrounding the crew with thick armour. Some anti-tank weapons work by making "scabs" of metal, called spall, fly off the inside of the vehicle. Spall flying around inside a vehicle is deadly. The passenger compartment of the US M113 APC is lined with a super-tough material called Kevlar to prevent spall.

Camouflage ▽

Most military vehicles are painted in colours that help them to blend in with their surroundings. Drab browns and greens are used to match soil and green plants. Lighter sandy browns are used in desert regions. This technique is called **camouflage**. Camouflage not only matches a vehicle's colour to its surrounding, it also breaks up the vehicle's shape and outline so that it's harder to identify. Netting and **foliage** are used to further break up a vehicle's shape and hide it from aircraft and ground forces.

▷ Engine power

A military vehicle's engine is designed to do everything a car engine does, but it also has to cope with the special problems of military service. Vehicle engines are designed to provide the most power in the smallest space. Military engines also have to be able to run non-stop all day without overheating, even when the vehicle is not moving. They have to be quick and easy to repair or to take out and replace.

Almost all large military land vehicles are powered by **diesel engines** because of their strength and reliability. A few military land vehicles use **gas turbines** similar to fighter-plane **jet engines**. Gas turbines pack even more power into a smaller space and they need less maintenance work to keep them going. Their main disadvantages are that they burn a lot of fuel, and they produce very hot **exhaust** gases that **heat-seeking missiles** can detect.

▽ Engine position

Most tanks have their engine at the back, but the designers of the Israeli Merkava tank put its engine at the front. One advantage of this design is that the engine gives the crew extra protection, like very thick **armour**. It also enabled the designers to put a door in the back of the tank, where the engine would normally be. In fighting conditions the crew can enter and leave the tank more safely through the back, instead of having to use the normal way through hatches on top.

Jet power ▽

The French Leclerc **MBT** is one of the few military land vehicles with a gas turbine engine. It uses it differently from the Abrams tank. Most of the time the Leclerc tank is powered by a 1,500-**horsepower** diesel engine. However, when it stops, the diesel engine is shut down and a small gas turbine is started to supply the tank with electrical power. This means that the tank's main engine does not need to be kept running when the tank is standing still.

LECLERC MBT

Crew: 3

Length: 9.9 metres

Weight: 54.5 tonnes

Top speed: 71 kph (44 mph)

Armament: 120 mm main gun
12.7 mm machine gun
7.62 mm anti-aircraft

This is the engine that powers the US M1 Abrams MBT.

Fuel ▷

Most engines are designed to burn only one type of fuel. Using a different fuel can damage the engine. Some military engines are designed to be able to burn several different fuels, so that they can use whatever is available. The US M1 Abrams and Russian T-90 tanks have multi-fuel engines that can burn a variety of fuels, including diesel oil, gasoline, and jet aircraft fuel.

Transporters

When an army goes to war, thousands of troops and thousands of tonnes of supplies have to be moved into position. An army's transport vehicles are as important as its weapons.

Military transport vehicles range from small people-carriers like jeeps to huge trucks for moving heavy cargo. They have to be able to go anywhere, so they usually have **all-wheel drive**. The wheels are fitted with deeply-grooved tyres to grip soft and loose surfaces. In some cases, the crew can even change the pressure of the air in the tyres from inside the cab. Letting some air out of the tyres lets them squash down onto the ground so that they give even better grip. The same vehicle can often be supplied with different bodies for carrying people, cargo, or weapons.

Multi-purpose vehicle ▽

The US Army's High Mobility Multi-purpose Wheeled Vehicle (HMMWV) is nicknamed the Humvee or Hummer. It is one of the most rugged and versatile light military vehicles in the world. It has four-wheel drive for maximum grip off-road and a high ground clearance for driving over rough ground. It can be transported by air and even dropped by parachute. Its designers have produced eleven different versions of the Humvee. These include general-purpose troop or cargo carriers, missile carriers, battlefield ambulances, and a version for towing **artillery** guns.

Cargo transport ▷

The M-939 truck is an army cargo transport truck. It can carry up to 5 tonnes of supplies on or off road at up to 105 kph (65 mph). It can also tow trailers or other vehicles weighing up to 9.5 tonnes. The basic truck can be supplied with six different bodies. It can also be fitted with a winch to pull itself, or another vehicle, out of trouble. By the late 1990s, the US Army had more than 30,000 M-939s.

OSHKOSH HEAVY EXPANDED MOBILITY TACTICAL TRUCK

Crew: 2

Length: 10.2 metres

Weight: 17.6 tonnes

Top speed: 100 kph (60 mph)

Heavy haulers ▽

The Oshkosh Heavy Expanded Mobility Tactical Truck (HEMTT) is designed to carry up to 10 tonnes of cargo wherever the US Army's tanks go. Its job is to keep the tanks and their crews supplied with everything they need to keep moving and fighting. All of its eight wheels are driven by its 445-**horsepower diesel engine**. It can even be driven through water up to 1.2 metres deep. More than 15,000 HEMTTs have been built since 1982.

Light armour

Troops are often sent to war-torn parts of the world to help keep the peace. If there is a strong likelihood of attack, they travel in **armoured** fighting vehicles (AFVs). A typical AFV weighs 15–20 tonnes and has a rotating gun turret similar to a tank's. An AFV designer has to decide whether to mount the vehicle on wheels or tank **tracks**. A tracked vehicle can move around easily on ground where a wheeled vehicle would get bogged down. However, a wheeled vehicle is faster than a tracked vehicle. The choice depends on how the vehicle is to be used.

Warrior ▽

The British Warrior AFV has lightweight **aluminium** armour that protects its soldiers against **shrapnel**, **mines**, and even small armour-piercing **rounds**. If it needs more protection, extra plates called appliqué armour can be added. It has enough room inside for a crew of three, plus up to seven soldiers. It can be used for **reconnaissance**, security patrols, rescue work, **artillery** command, and resupply duties. It can be fitted with a range of weapons, from machine guns to **mortars** and missiles.

WARRIOR AFV

Crew: 3 + 7 troops

Length: 6.3 metres

Weight: 24 tonnes

Top speed: 75 kph (47 mph)

Armament: 30 mm cannon
7.62 mm machine gun
2 x missile launchers

The French ERC 90 F1 Lynx armoured vehicle is unusual. It can be equipped with special water-jets designed to propel it through water at around 7 kph (5 mph).

△ Water power

Some armoured fighting vehicles are light enough to float across rivers. Their hulls are specially designed to be watertight. However, their designers do not usually fit them with any special equipment to propel them through water – they just use their tracks. Tracks are not designed for propulsion in water, but they "catch" the water just enough to move a vehicle slowly.

Future light armour ▽

The next generation of light-armour vehicles is now being designed. The European Boxer Multi-Role Armoured Vehicle (MRAV) is a "modular" vehicle. This means it is a vehicle made from a series of parts, or **modules**. These can be put together in different ways to create different versions of the vehicle. The base vehicle is an **eight-wheel-drive chassis**. A "mission module" is then fitted to this. The choice of module depends on the type of mission. One mission module can be replaced by another one in less than an hour.

Long-range firepower

During a battle, ground forces may have to attack targets tens or hundreds of kilometres away. **Self-propelled howitzers** and rocket launchers are designed to do exactly this.

Tanks attack targets their crews can see, up to about 5,000 metres away. Howitzers can raise their longer **barrels** higher and hurl a **shell** up to 30–40 kilometres away. For targets even further away, a different type of weapon is needed. Instead of blasting a shell out of a barrel, self-propelled launch vehicles fire rocket-propelled **warheads** up to several hundred kilometres. Self-propelled guns are designed to move into position quickly, fire their shells or rockets, and then move quickly away. As these vehicles normally operate behind the front line, they don't need the heavy **armour** of a **MBT**. Being light, with little armour, makes them more **manoeuvrable**.

Howitzers ▷

The US M109A6 Paladin looks like a tank, but it is actually a self-propelled howitzer designed to hit targets up to 30 kilometres away.

- Its main weapon is a 155-mm cannon.

- Its 440-**horsepower diesel engine** can move the 29-tonne **tracked** vehicle at up to 64 kph (40 mph).

- It can fire its first **round** within 60 seconds of coming to a halt.

- There is enough space inside the armoured hull for a commander, driver, gunner, loader, and 39 rounds of ammunition.

◁ Multiple launch rocket system

The Multiple Launch Rocket System (MLRS) is a tracked vehicle armed with twelve **surface-to-surface** rockets or missiles. The launching tubes are mounted on a modified Bradley M2 armoured fighting vehicle **chassis**. The chassis had to be made longer to carry the rocket launcher. Target information is transmitted to the vehicle's computer, which aims the rockets and tells the crew when they are ready to be fired. The MLRS can fire rockets and missiles with ranges from 15 kilometres up to about 300 kilometres.

Rockets on wheels ▽

The High Mobility **Artillery** Rocket System (HIMARS) is a mobile rocket launcher developed in the USA. It has the same firepower as the Multiple Launch Rocket System (MLRS), but it moves on wheels instead of tracks. It is about half the weight of MLRS, so it can move faster. It can get into position, fire, and move away before its launch site can be located and attacked. HIMARS is designed to fit inside a C-130 transport plane. It entered service in 2005.

HIGH-MOBILITY ARTILLERY ROCKET SYSTEM (HIMARS)

Crew: 3

Length: 7.0 metres

Weight: 10.9 tonnes

Top speed: 85 kph (53 mph)

Protecting the column

Military forces can be attacked from the air at any time. Vehicles have been specially designed to detect air attacks and fight them off.

Tanks and **armoured** fighting vehicles (AFVs) travel with troops and supply **convoys** to protect them. Whenever possible, helicopters and fighters also give air cover. There are also specially designed air-defence vehicles. **Radar** vehicles search the sky for incoming enemy aircraft. **Self-propelled** anti-aircraft guns and air-defence vehicles armed with missiles fight them off. Attacks may come from ground forces, too, so ground and air **reconnaissance** vehicles keep a good look out.

Anti-aircraft ▽ guns

The Ukrainian ZSU-23-4 Shilka is a self-propelled anti-aircraft gun. It rides on a **chassis** with **tracks**. It has **stabilized guns** so it can fire on the move. A radar dish mounted on top detects and tracks targets on the ground and in the air. The targets may be stationary, such as missile launchers, or moving, such as ground vehicles or aircraft in flight. Targets picked up by the radar are then attacked by four automatic cannon on the turret.

ZSU-23-4 SHILKA ANTI-AIRCRAFT VEHICLE	
Crew:	4
Length:	6.5 metres
Weight:	20.5 tonnes
Top speed:	50 kph (31 mph)
Armament:	4 x 23-mm anti-aircraft guns

Air defence ▷

The same weapon system can be mounted on different types of vehicles. The Roland air-defence missile system is designed to deal with low-flying enemy aircraft. It can be mounted on its own truck for maximum mobility or on a towed trailer. A radar dish on top locates targets up to 20 kilometres away. It tracks them until they come within the missiles' range of 6, 8, or 11 kilometres. Two missiles are carried ready to fire, with another eight stored inside.

Planes without pilots ▽

Spying on enemy forces from aircraft is very dangerous because of the risk of being shot down. So, Unmanned Aerial Vehicles (UAVs) are increasingly being used. They are designed to circle over the enemy for hours or even days, sending pictures directly to commanders and front-line troops. There are two types of UAVs:

- Remotely Piloted Vehicles (RPVs), like the US Predator, are flown from the ground by a pilot who has a control panel.

- Newly developed UAVs, such as the US Global Hawk, are more advanced. Once programmed with a mission, Global Hawk takes off, flies the mission, and lands itself automatically.

The US Global Hawk unmanned spy-plane flew its first military mission over Afghanistan in 2001.

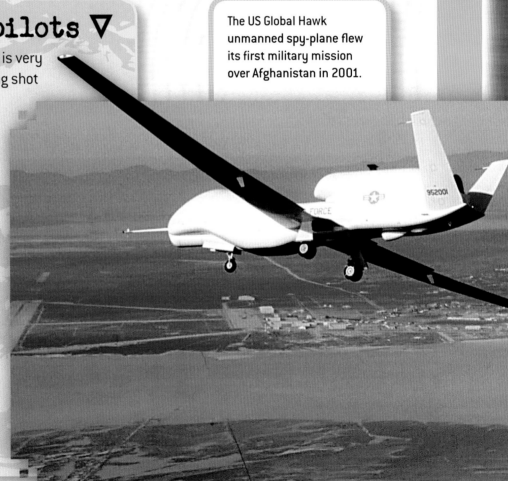

▷ Special vehicles

Military forces use many of the same vehicles that are used in the construction industry, including diggers, loaders, dump-trucks, cranes, and bulldozers, plus some more specialized vehicles. These special-purpose vehicles include bridge layers and **armoured** recovery vehicles. Bridge-laying vehicles put temporary bridges in place. The fastest of them can span a gap for troops and vehicles to cross within a few minutes. Some of these vehicles are built by converting tanks.

Some military transport work also requires specially designed vehicles. Recovery vehicles have to be able to go anywhere, so that they can lift or pull other vehicles out of trouble. **Main battle tanks**, on the other hand, can be driven on roads, but they are so heavy that their **tracks** can cause a lot of damage to the road surface. For this reason, they are often transported on trailers.

◁ Laying bridges

The Wolverine Heavy Assault Bridge System is built on an M1 Abrams tank **chassis**.

- It can lay a bridge strong enough to carry a battle tank over a 24-metre gap in less than five minutes.

- The bridge is carried in four sections on top of the vehicle.

- **Hydraulic** arms assemble the bridge and slide it out over the gap.

Recovery vehicles △

Military vehicles can operate in very difficult conditions, but they do sometimes break down or get bogged down in soft ground. When they do, and if they are worth rescuing, recovery vehicles are sent to pull them out. They are equipped with winches and sometimes a crane to lift or drag another vehicle. Some recovery vehicles are based on wheeled trucks. The biggest and heaviest are built on a tank chassis with tracks. Recovery vehicles based on tanks carry the thickest armour and so can operate in more dangerous combat conditions.

A vehicle as heavy as a main battle tank needs an equally powerful recovery vehicle to come to its aid.

Transporting tanks ▽

The US Oshkosh M1070 Heavy Equipment Transporter (HET) has the important job of moving the heaviest military loads. It can even carry Abrams battle tanks. The M1070 HET is an **eight-wheel-drive tractor unit** that pulls a trailer carrying the load. The whole rig can weigh up to 105 tonnes when fully loaded. Such an enormously heavy vehicle needs a very powerful engine to haul its load on the level and up slopes. It is powered by a 500-**horsepower**, 12-litre, **turbocharged diesel engine**.

OSHKOSH M1070 HEAVY EQUIPMENT TRANSPORTER

Crew: 2 (+ 4 passengers)

Length: 9.2 metres

Weight: 18.5 tonnes

Top speed:
70 kph (45 mph) unloaded
50 kph (30 mph) fully loaded

Data files

This table of information compares the basic specifications of some of today's military vehicles.

Vehicle	Country of origin	Length (metres)	Weight (tonnes)	Top speed (kph / mph)	Main gun (mm)
Abrams M1A2 MBT	USA	9.8	69.5	67 / 42	120
Bradley M2 AFV	USA	6.5	22.5	66 / 41	25
Challenger 2 MBT	UK	11.5	62.5	59 / 37	120
HIMARS rocket system	USA	7.0	10.9	85 / 53	none
Leclerc MBT	France	9.9	54.5	71 / 44	120
Leopard 2 MBT	Germany	7.7	62.0	72 / 45	120
Merkava MBT	Israel	8.8	60.0	46 / 28	120
Oshkosh M977 HEMTT	USA	10.2	17.6	100 / 60	none
Oshkosh M1070 Transporter	USA	9.2	18.5	70 / 45	none
Paladin M109A6 Howitzer	USA	9.7	28.9	64 / 40	155
Stormer 30 light tank	UK	5.25	13.0	80 / 50	30
Strv-103 MBT	Sweden	9.0	42.5	50 / 31	105
T-90 MBT	Russia	9.5	46.5	65 / 40	125
Warrior armoured vehicle	UK	6.3	24.0	75 / 47	30
ZSU-23-4 anti-aircraft vehicle	Ukraine	6.5	20.5	50 / 31	4 x 23

Leonardo's tank ▷

The great Italian artist, sculptor, engineer, and scientist, Leonardo da Vinci (1452–1519), made many drawings of machines that were far ahead of their time. Among them, there is a strange contraption that looks like a huge metal pie dish. It rides on four wheels and cannon point out in all directions. It is a battle tank, designed more than 400 years before the first tank was actually built!

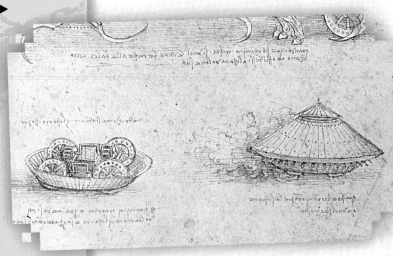

Further information

Books

M1A1 Abrams Tank, David Baker (Rourke Publishing, 2007)
Tanks, George Forty (J H Haynes & Co, 2007)
US Army Infantry Fighting Vehicles, Martha E. H. Rustad (Blazers, 2006)
Mega Book of Tanks, Lynne Gibbs (Chrysalis Children's Books, 2005)
US Army Fighting Vehicles, Richard Bartlett (Heinemann Library, 2003)

Websites

http://www.armytankmuseum.com.au
The website of the Royal Australian Armoured Corps Tank Museum.

http://www.tankmuseum.com
The website of the Tank Museum in Bovington, England.

http://www.army-technology.com/projects
A US website with lots of information about tanks and other military vehicles.

http://en.wikipedia.org/wiki/History_of_the_tank
The history of tanks.

The first tank ▽

The first practical tank was the British Mark I, built during the First World War. It was called a "tank" to make it sound like a water tank and keep its real purpose secret. The Mark I weighed 28.5 tonnes. Its top speed was only 4.5 kph. Its guns were mounted in its sides. Mark Is were used for the first time on 15 September 1916, at the Battle of the Somme.

Glossary

all-wheel drive a method of increasing a vehicle's grip on the ground by powering all of its wheels

aluminium a lightweight metal used in vehicle construction

amphibious designed to be used on land and in water

armour thick plates of metal or other materials that protect military vehicles

armoured personnel carrier (APC) vehicle, protected by armour, used to carry troops safely under fire

artillery large calibre guns or cannon that fire shells over long distances

barrel the long tube through which a gun fires its bullets or artillery shells

camouflage a method for making a vehicle more difficult to see or identify. Coloured paint or netting is used to make it blend into its surroundings.

chassis the main frame of a military vehicle that the rest of the vehicle is built on

convoy a group of vehicles travelling together

covering fire shooting at enemy troops to stop them from attacking friendly troops while they are entering or leaving vehicles or moving around in the open

dense tightly packed. A dense material like uranium has very tightly packed particles of matter, making it very heavy and more difficult to penetrate.

depleted uranium a type of heavy, dense metal left over when fuel for some nuclear power stations or atomic bombs is made. Its weight makes it ideal for punching holes through armoured vehicles.

diesel engine a type of engine that burns a fuel called diesel oil. Diesel engines are used by many military vehicles because they are tough and reliable.

eight-wheel drive a system that connects a vehicle's engine to all eight of its wheels, so that all eight wheels are driven simultaneously

exhaust the hot gases given out by an engine

foliage a plant's leaves

gas turbine a jet engine used to power some military vehicles

heat-seeking missile weapon that hits a target by detecting the heat it gives out and flying towards it

horsepower (hp) an ability to do work that is roughly equal to the work that one horse can do, or about 746 watts of electrical power

howitzer artillery weapon that can raise its short- or medium-length barrel to a steep angle

hydraulic operated by the pressure of a liquid forced through pipes

jet engine another name for a gas turbine, a type of engine used by some military vehicles

laser a device that produces an intense beam of light

light tank lightly armed and armoured vehicle, often used for reconnaissance

main battle tank (MBT) biggest and most powerful of an army's tanks

manoeuvre move or steer in a planned way

mines explosive devices laid on, or under, the ground so that they explode when a vehicle drives over them or someone steps on them

module a small part used with other modules to create a tank

mortar small cannon with a short barrel

nuclear to do with nuclei, the particles at the centre of atoms. Nuclear weapons use energy released from atomic nuclei.

periscope a device that uses mirrors or prisms (triangular blocks of glass) to let someone see something that isn't in the direct line of sight

radar Radio Detection And Ranging, a method of finding distant objects by sending out radio waves and picking up any reflections that bounce back

radioactive having or giving out radiation

range-finder a device for finding out how far away an object is

reconnaissance obtaining information about an enemy's activities

round single bullet, artillery shell, or tank shell

self-propelled gun that has its own engine and so does not need to be towed by another vehicle

shells hollow metal cases filled with explosives and fired from a gun

shrapnel shell fragments; pieces of metal that fly out from an exploding shell

stabilized gun gun that keeps its barrel pointing at a target even if the tank carrying the gun is turning or driving over rough ground

surface-to-surface a type of missile that is fired from a vehicle on the ground at targets that are also on the ground

throttle the part of an engine that varies the amount of fuel or air, or both, that flow into the engine. When a vehicle's driver presses the accelerator pedal, the throttle opens and the engine speeds up.

torsion twisting

tracks flexible metal bands made from a series of links, like bicycle chains, that are fitted to some military vehicles, especially tanks. Tracks enable a vehicle to be driven over soft ground without slipping or sinking.

tractor unit the part of an articulated truck that contains the engine and pulls the trailer

turbocharged boosted in power by a turbocharger. A turbocharger forces extra air into an engine to burn more fuel and produce more power.

warheads the explosive parts of missiles

welded joined by melting the parts that meet so that they fuse together as one

Index